KEYBOARD CHORD SONG BOOK

Today's Smash Hits

GW00370490

Wise Publications
London/New York/Sydney/Paris/Copenhagen/Madrid/Tokyo

Exclusive distributors:
Music Sales Limited
8/9 Frith Street,
London W1D 3JB, England.
Music Sales Pty Limited
120 Rothschild Avenue
Rosebery, NSW 2018,
Australia.

Order No. AM962830
ISBN 0-7119-8044-6
This book © Copyright 2000 by Wise Publications

Book design by Chloë Alexander
Music arranged & engraved by Roger Day
Compiled by Nick Crispin

Photographs courtesy of London Features International

Printed in the United Kingdom by
Printwise (Haverhill) Limited, Haverhill, Suffolk.

Your Guarantee of Quality
As publishers, we strive to produce every book to the highest
commercial standards. The music has been freshly engraved and
the book has been carefully designed to minimise awkward page
turns and to make playing from it a real pleasure. Particular care
has been given to specifying acid-free, neutral-sized paper made
from pulps which have not been elemental chlorine bleached. This
pulp is from farmed sustainable forests and was produced with
special regard for the environment. Throughout, the printing and
binding have been planned to ensure a sturdy, attractive
publication which should give years of enjoyment. If your copy
fails to meet our high standards, please inform us and we will
gladly replace it.

Music Sales' complete catalogue describes thousands of titles and
is available in full colour sections by subject, direct from Music
Sales Limited. Please state your areas of interest and send a
cheque/postal order for £1.50 for postage to: Music Sales Limited,
Newmarket Road, Bury St. Edmunds, Suffolk IP33 3YB.

www.musicsales.com

American Pie

Words & Music by Don McLean

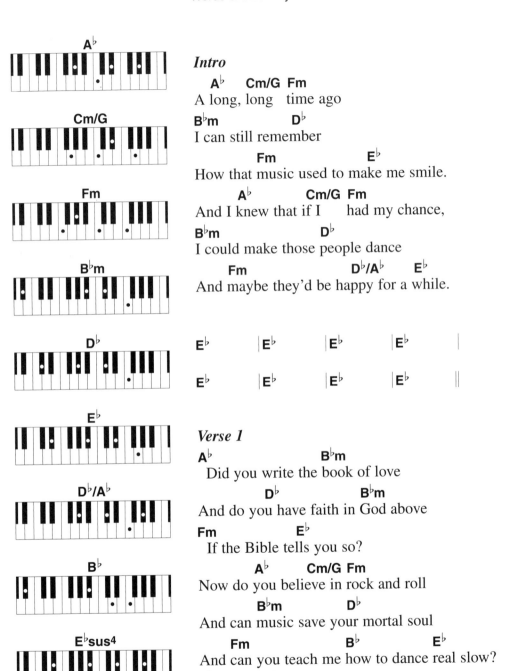

Intro

  A♭   **Cm/G** **Fm**
A long, long time ago

B♭m   **D♭**
I can still remember

       Fm   **E♭**
How that music used to make me smile.

       A♭   **Cm/G** **Fm**
And I knew that if I   had my chance,

B♭m   **D♭**
I could make those people dance

       Fm   **D♭/A♭**   **E♭**
And maybe they'd be happy for a while.

E♭ |**E♭** |**E♭** |**E♭** |

E♭ |**E♭** |**E♭** |**E♭** ||

Verse 1

A♭   **B♭m**
  Did you write the book of love

            D♭   **B♭m**
And do you have faith in God above

Fm   **E♭**
  If the Bible tells you so?

          A♭   **Cm/G Fm**
Now do you believe in rock and roll

         B♭m   **D♭**
And can music save your mortal soul

        Fm   **B♭**   **E♭**
And can you teach me how to dance real slow?

E♭sus⁴ **E♭**

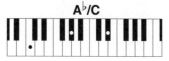

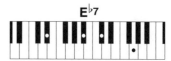

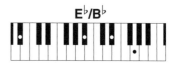

Bridge 1

          Fm   E♭
Well I know that you're in love with him
          Fm   E♭
Cos I   saw you dancing in the gym,
          D♭   A♭/C   B♭m
You both kicked off your shoes,

(Both kicked off your shoes.)
          D♭   E♭
Man, I dig those rhythm and blues.
          A♭   Cm/G Fm
I was a lonely teenage broncin' buck
          B♭m   D♭
With a pink carnation and a pick-up truck,
          A♭   E♭/G   Fm
But I   knew that I was out of luck
          D♭   E♭7   A♭   D♭
The day the music died.
A♭   E♭
  I started singing

Chorus 1

A♭   D♭   A♭   E♭
Bye, bye Miss American Pie,
          A♭   D♭   A♭   E♭
Drove my Chevy to the levee but the levee was dry.
          A♭   D♭   A♭   E♭
Them good ole boys were drinkin' whiskey and rye,
          Fm   B♭
Singin' "This will be the day that I die,
Fm   E♭   E♭/D♭ │A♭/C   E♭/B♭
This will be the day that I die."
E♭   E♭/D♭ │A♭/C   E♭/B♭

Verse 2

A♭   B♭m
  I met a girl who sang the blues
          D♭   B♭m
And I asked her for some happy news.
Fm   E♭
  But she just smiled and turned away.

$A^\flat$ **Cm/G** **Fm**
Well I went down to the sacred store
      $B^\flat m$ $D^\flat$
Where I'd heard the music years before,
     Fm $B^\flat$ $E^\flat$ $E^\flat$sus4 $E^\flat$
But the man there said the music wouldn't play.

Bridge 2

        Fm $E^\flat$
Well now, in the streets the children screamed,
    Fm $E^\flat$
The lovers cried and the poets dreamed,
   $D^\flat$ $A^\flat$/**C** $B^\flat m$
But not a word was spoken,
    $D^\flat$ $E^\flat$
The church bells all were broken.
       $A^\flat$ **Cm/G** **Fm**
And the three men I   ad--mire the most,
   $B^\flat m$ $D^\flat$
The Father, Son and Holy Ghost,
    $A^\flat$ $E^\flat$/**G**   **Fm**
They   caught the last train for the coast
     $D^\flat$ $E^\flat 7$ $A^\flat$ $D^\flat$
The day the music died.
$A^\flat$ $E^\flat$
  We started singing

Chorus 2

Repeat Chorus 1

$|E^\flat 7$ $|E^\flat 7$ $|E^\flat 7$ $|E^\flat 7$ $|E^\flat 7$ $|E^\flat 7$ $|E^\flat 7$ $|E^\flat 7$ $||$
die."

Chorus 3

Repeat Chorus 1

$E^\flat$ $E^\flat$/$D^\flat$
die."

Ending

$\|$: $A^\flat$/**C** $E^\flat$/$B^\flat$ $E^\flat$ $E^\flat$/$D^\flat$:$\|$ *Play 3 times*
   We started singing,
$A^\flat$/**C** $E^\flat$/$B^\flat$
   We started singing.

Babylon

Words & Music by David Gray

E♭

B♭

Intro

|N.C. | | | |

|E♭ |B♭ |Fm7 |B♭7   B♭6   ‖

Fm7

B♭7

Verse 1

E♭maj9/G
Friday night and I'm goin' nowhere,

A♭maj7   E♭maj9/G   A♭maj7
All the lights are changin' green to red.

E♭maj9/G
Turnin' over T.V. stations,

A♭maj7   E♭maj9/G   A♭maj7
Situations runnin' through my head.

E♭maj9
Lookin' back through time,

         A♭add9/C   B♭11
You know it's clear that I've been blind,

      E♭maj9 |A♭add9/C   B♭11
I've been a fool

      E♭maj9
To open up my heart

      A♭add9/C   B♭11
To all that jealousy, that bitterness,

   E♭maj9 |A♭add9/C   B♭11
That ridicule.

B♭6

E♭maj9/G

A♭maj7

E♭maj9

A♭add9/C

B♭11

more chords overleaf…

Gm7

A♭

Chorus 1

E♭   B♭
  An' if you want it, come an' get it,

Fm7   Gm7
  For cryin' out loud.

E♭   B♭
  The love that I was givin' you

     Fm7   A♭
Was   never in doubt.

E♭   B♭   Fm7
  Let go your heart, let go your head

     B♭7   B♭6
And feel it now.

E♭   B♭   Fm7
  Let go your heart, let go your head

     B♭
And feel it now,

      E♭ A♭maj7   E♭   A♭maj7
Babylon,   Babylon.

Verse 2

E♭maj9/G
Saturday an' I'm runnin' wild

    A♭maj7   E♭maj9/G   A♭maj7
An' all the lights are changin' red to green.

E♭maj9/G
Movin' through the crowds, I'm pushin',

A♭maj7   E♭maj9/G   A♭maj7
Chemicals are rushin' in my bloodstream.

     E♭maj9
Only wish that you were here,

      A♭add9/C   B♭11
You know I'm seein' it so clear,

    E♭maj9 | A♭add9/C   B♭11
I've been afraid

     E♭maj9
To show you how I really feel,

   A♭add9/C   B♭11   E♭maj9
Admit to some o' those bad mistakes

     | A♭add9/C   B♭11
I've made.

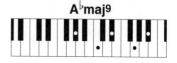

A♭maj9

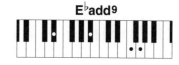

E♭add9

Chorus 2

E♭   **B♭**
 Well if you want it, come an' get it,

Fm7   **Gm7**
  For cryin' out loud.

E♭   **B♭**
 The love that I was   givin' you

     Fm7   **A♭**
Was   never in doubt.

E♭   **B♭**   **Fm7**
 Let go your heart, let go your head

      B♭7   **B♭6**
And feel it now.

E♭   **B♭**   **Fm7**
 Let go your heart, let go your head

      B♭7   **B♭6**
And feel it now.

E♭   **B♭**   **Fm7**
 Let go your heart, let go your head

      B♭
And feel__ it.

E♭   **B♭**   **Fm7**
 Let go your heart, let go your head

      B♭
And feel it now,

     E♭ **A♭maj9**   **E♭** **A♭maj7**
Babylon,   Babylon.

    E♭add9 A♭maj7   **E♭** **A♭maj7**
Babylon,   Babylon.

      E♭   **A♭maj7**   **N.C.**
Babylon, why, why, why, why, why, why?

Bag It Up

Words & Music by Geri Halliwell, Andy Watkins & Paul Wilson

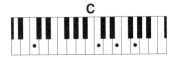
C

Dm7

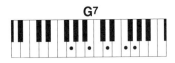
G7

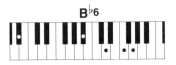
B♭6

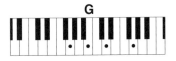
G

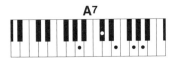
A7

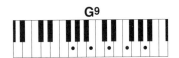
G9

Intro

C   N.C. | | | ‖
(Treat him like a lady.)   Uh-huh, uh-huh!
|Dm7 |G7 |Dm7 |G7 B♭6 ‖

Verse 1

Dm7
I like choc'late and controversy,

He likes Fridays and bad company.

I like midnight, it's when I'm in the mood,

But he likes the morning, that's when he's rude.

Bridge 1

G   Dm7
 Just a bad case of opposite sex,
G   Dm7
 Have to look to the stars.
G   Dm7
 All we need is a little respect
   G7   A7
Cos men are from Venus and girls are from Mars.

Chorus 1

Dm7
Bag it up, don't drop the baby.
G9
Boot him out, no buts or maybe.
Dm7
Wind him up and make him crazy,
G7   B♭6
Whoa, whoa, whoa, whoa.

Dm⁷
Take him back, don't drop the baby.
G⁹
Spin him out, not buts or maybe.
Dm⁷
Do your thing, come on lady,
G⁷   **B♭6**   **Dm⁷** | **G⁷**
Whoa, whoa, whoa, whoa, lady.
Dm⁷ | **G⁷** **B♭6** ‖

Verse 2
Dm⁷
I don't take sugar on my colour TV,

Yet he likes it loaded with eye candy.

I neeed some space and he needs a room,

But then he keeps me waiting by leaving too soon.

Bridge 2

As Bridge 1

Chorus 2

As Chorus 1

Yeah.

Link
G⁷   **Dm⁷**   **G⁷**
Ooh, yeah! Ooh, yeah! Ooh, yeah!
Dm⁷
Treat him like a lady!
G⁷
Treat him like a lady!
Dm⁷   **G⁷**
Tease him, please him, chase me, yeah!

Chorus 3

As Chorus 1

Repeat to fade

Go Let It Out

Words & Music by Noel Gallagher

A7

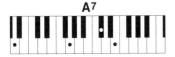

D/A

Fadd9

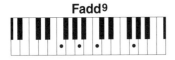

G

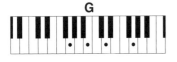

D

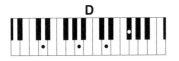

A

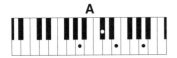

Intro

        A7 | ||

Two, three, four.

Verse 1

A7
Paint no illusion,

Try to click with what you got.

Taste every potion,

Cos if you like yourself a lot,

Chorus 1

         D/A   **Fadd9**
Go let it out, go let it in
G   **A7**
  And go let it out.

(Pick up the bass.)

Verse 2

A7
Life is precocious

In the most peculiar way.

Sister Psychosis

Don't got a lot to say.

Chorus 2

    D   **Fadd9**
She go let it out, she go let it in,
G   **A**
 She go let it out.
     D   **Fadd9**
She go let it out, she go let it in,
G   **A7**
 She go let it out.

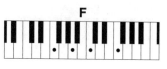

Middle 1

D **F**   **A**   **C6/9**
 Is it any wonder why princes and kings
D   **F**   **A**   **C6/9**
 Are clowns that caper in their sawdust rings?
D **F**   **A**   **C6/9**
 Ordinary people that are like you and me,
    G7   **D5**
We're the keepers of their destiny.
    G7   **D5** **A7** |**A7**
We're the keepers of their destiny. Ooh!

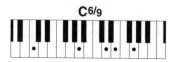

Verse 3

    A7
I'm goin' leavin' the city,

I'm goin' drivin' outta town.

And you're comin' with me,

The right time is always now.

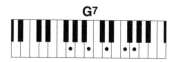

Chorus 3

    D   **Fadd9**
So go let it out, and go let it in
G   **A**
 And go let it out.
    D   **Fadd9**
So go let it out, so go let it in
G   **A7**
 And go let it out.

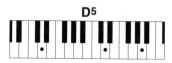

more chords overleaf...

Dsus⁴

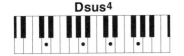

D⁵add¹¹

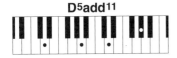

Middle 2

D   F   A   C⁶/₉
  Is it any wonder why princes and kings

D   F   A   C⁶/₉
  Are clowns that caper in their sawdust rings?

D   F   A   C⁶/₉
  Ordinary people that are like you and me,

          G⁷   D⁵
We're the builders of their destiny.

          G⁷   D⁵
We're the builders of their destiny.

          G⁷   D⁵
We're the builders of their destiny.

          G⁷
We're the builders of their destiny.

Link

| D Dsus⁴ | D⁵add¹¹ Dsus⁴ | D Dsus⁴ | D⁵add¹¹ Dsus⁴ |

| D Dsus⁴ | D⁵add¹¹ Dsus⁴ | D Dsus⁴ | D⁵add¹¹ |

Chorus 4

               D   C⁶/₉
So go let it out, go let it in,

G   D   C⁶/₉
  Go let it out, don't let it in.

G   D   C⁶/₉
  And go let it out, go let it in,

G   D
  Go let it out, don't let it in,

C⁶/₉   G
Don't let it in, don't let it in.

Outro

‖: D | C⁶/₉   G   :‖ *Play 4 times*

‖: D⁵ | D⁵   :‖ *Repeat to fade*

It Feels So Good

Words & Music by Sonique, Linus Burdick & Simon Belofsky

Fm

Intro

| Fm | | Fm | | D♭/F | | D♭/F | ‖ |

D♭/F

Verse 1

Fm
You always make me smile
D♭/F
When I'm feeling down.
B♭/F
You give me such a vibe,
      Fm
It's totally bona fide, mm.
Fm
It's not the way you walk
      D♭/F
And it ain't the way you talk,
B♭/F
It ain't the job you got
      Fm
That keeps me satisfied.

B♭/F

E♭

Chorus 1

      E♭
(Your love, it feels so good.)

      Fm
And that's what takes me high,
      E♭
(Higher than I've been before.)
      Fm
Your live, it keeps me alive,
      E♭
(Thought I should let you know)
      Fm
That your touch, it means so much.

$E^\flat$
(When I'm alone at night)

Fm
It's you I'm always thinkin' of.

Ooh baby.

Link 1

	Fm		Fm		$D^\flat$/F		$D^\flat$/F		
	$B^\flat$/F		$B^\flat$/F		$D^\flat$/F		$D^\flat$/F			

Verse 2

Fm
Ooh, I want you

$D^\flat$/F
To understand

$B^\flat$/F
How I feel, yeah,

Fm
Deep inside.

Fm
Oh, you made me feel

     $D^\flat$/F
What I need to feel,

$B^\flat$/F
Yes,

     Fm
In my heart.

Chorus 2

As Chorus 1

Link 2

	Fm		Fm		$D^\flat$/F		$D^\flat$/F		
	$B^\flat$/F		$B^\flat$/F		Fm		Fm			

Chorus 3

$E^\flat$
(Your love, it feels so good.)

Fm
And that's what takes me high,

$E^\flat$
(Higher than I've been before.)

Fm
Your love, it keeps me alive,

$E^\flat$
(Thought I should let you know)

Fm
That your touch, it means so much.

$E^\flat$
(When I'm alone at night)

Fm
It's you I'm always thinking of.

Ooh baby.

Chorus 4

$\mathbf{\|{:}}$

$E^\flat$
(Your love, it feels so good.)

Fm
And that's what takes me high,

$E^\flat$
(Higher than I've been before.)

Fm
Your love, it keeps me alive,

$E^\flat$
(Thought I should let you know)

Fm
That your touch, it means so much.

$E^\flat$
(When I'm alone at night)

Fm
It's you I'm always thinking of.

$\mathbf{{:}\|}$ *Repeat to fade*
Ooh baby.

I Have A Dream

Words and Music by Benny Andersson & Björn Ulvaeus

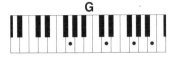

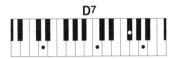

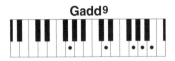

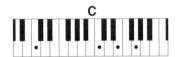

Intro

G | | |

D7 | |G |

Verse 1

           D7   Gadd9
I have a dream, a song to sing,
            D7   G
To help me cope with everything.
               D7   G
If you see the wonder of a fairy tale,
             D7   G
You can take the future even if you fail.

Chorus 1

          D7
I believe in angels,
                 C   G
Something good in everything I see.
          D7
I believe in angels,
               C   G
When I know the time is right for me.
          D7
I'll cross the stream,
        G |G
I have a dream.

Verse 2

      D7   **Gadd9**
I have a dream, a fantasy,
         D7   **G**
To help me through reality.
            D7   **G**
And my destination makes it worth the while,
               D7   **G**
Pushing through the darkness, still another mile.

Chorus 2

As Chorus 1

D7 | | **G**

Verse 3

      D7   **Gadd9**
I have a dream, a song to sing,
         D7   **G**
To help me cope with everything.
           D7   **G**
If you see the wonder of a fairy tale,
         D7   **G**
You can take the future even if you fail.

Chorus 3

As Chorus 1

Ending

         D7
I'll cross the stream,
    G | | | **D7** | | **G**   ‖
I have a dream.

Keep On Movin'

Words & Music by Richard Stannard, Julian Gallagher,
Richard Breen, Sean Conlon & Jason Brown

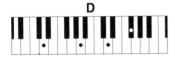

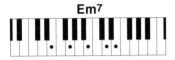

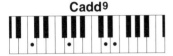

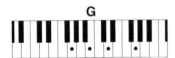

Intro

| D | Em⁷ | Cadd⁹ | G | |

| D | Em⁷ | Cadd⁹ | G | ‖

Verse 1

    D   Em⁷
I woke up today with this feelin'
       Cadd⁹   G
That better things are coming my way.
       D   Em⁷
And if the sunshine has a meaning,
             Cadd⁹   G
It's telling me not to let things get in my way.

Bridge 1

D
  When the rainy days are dying,

Em⁷
  Gotta keep on, keep on trying.

Cadd⁹
  All the bees and birds are flying.

G
(Ah.)

D
  Never let go, gotta hold on in

Em⁷
  Non-stop till the break of dawnin',

Cadd⁹
  Keep movin', don't stop rockin'.

G
(Ah.)

Chorus 1

    D   **Em⁷**

Get on up when you're down,

     Cadd⁹   **G**

Baby, take a good look around.

        D   **Em⁷**

I know it's not much, but it's O.K.

       Cadd⁹   **G**   **|D N.C.**

We'll keep on movin' on anyway.

Verse 2

D   **Em⁷**

Feels like I should be screamin',

Cadd⁹   **G**

Tryin' to get it through to my friends.

    D   **Em⁷**

Sometimes it feels that life has no meaning.

       Cadd⁹   **G**

But I know things will be alright in the end.

Bridge 2

As Bridge 1

Chorus 2

As Chorus 1

Bridge 3

As Bridge 1

Chorus 3

‖:   **D**   **Em⁷**

 Get on up when you're down,

     Cadd⁹   **G**

Baby, take a good look around.

        D   **Em⁷**

I know it's not much, but it's O.K.

       Cadd⁹   **G**   **:‖** *Repeat to fade*

We'll keep on movin' on anyway.

Man! I Feel Like A Woman!

Words & Music by Shania Twain & R. J. Lange

B♭5

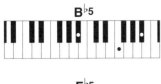

E♭5

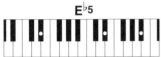

Intro

Let's go, girls!

| B♭5 | B♭5 | B♭5 | B♭5 | ‖

Verse 1

    B♭5
I'm going out tonight,

I'm feelin' alright,
                    E♭5   **B♭5**
Gonna let it all hang out.

Wanna make some noise,

Really raise my voice,
                        E♭5   **B♭5**
Yeah, I wanna scream and shout.
B♭5
      Ah!

Verse 2

    B♭5
No inhibitions,

Make no conditions,
                  E♭5   **B♭5**
Get a little outta line.

I ain't gonna act

Politically correct,
                    E♭5
I only wanna have a good time.

Bridge 1

A♭
　The best thing about being a woman

B♭
　Is the prerogative to have a little fun and…

Chorus 1

F
　Oh, oh, oh,

Go totally crazy,

Forget I'm a lady.

Men's shirts, short skirts.

Oh, oh, oh
Dm
　Really go wild, yeah,
B♭　　　　**F**
Doin' it in style.

Oh, oh, oh,

Get in the action,

Feel the attraction.

Colour my hair, do what I dare.

Oh, oh, oh,
Dm
　I wanna be free, yeah
　　B♭　　　　　**Gm⁷**
To feel the way I feel.
N.C.
Man! I feel like a woman!

Link
| **B**♭**5** | | **B**♭**5** | | **B**♭**5** | | **E**♭**5** | | ‖ |

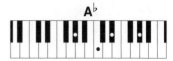

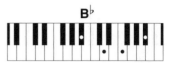

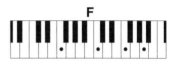

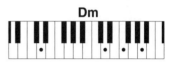

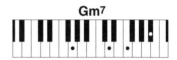

more chords overleaf…

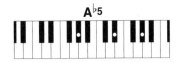

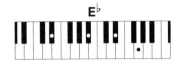

Verse 3

B♭5

The girls need a break,

Tonight we're gonna take

         E♭5 B♭5

The chance to get out on the town.

We don't need romance,

We only wanna dance,

        E♭5

We're gonna let our hair hang down.

Bridge 2

As Bridge 1

Chorus 2

As Chorus 1

Middle

|B♭5 |E♭5 |B♭5 |B♭5 |

|A♭5 |E♭5 |B♭5 |B♭5   ‖

Bridge 3

A♭

 The best thing about being a woman

B♭   N.C.

 Is the prerogative to have a little fun and…fun, fun!

Chorus 3

F
   Oh, oh, oh,

Go totally crazy,

Forget I'm a lady.

Men's shirts, short skirts.

Oh, oh, oh
Dm
  Really go wild, yeah,
B♭   **F**
Doin' it in style.

Oh, oh, oh,

Get in the action,

Feel the attraction.

Colour my hair, do what I dare.

Oh, oh, oh,
Dm
   I wanna be free, yeah
   B♭   **Gm7**
To feel the way I feel.

(Feel the way I feel.)
N.C.
Man! I feel like a woman!

Outro

|**B♭** |**B♭** |**A♭** |**E♭** |

|**B♭** |**B♭** |**A♭** |

E♭   **B♭5**
  I feel like a woman!

Never Be The Same Again

Words & Music by Melanie Chisholm, Rhett Lawrence, Paul F. Cruz,
Lisa Lopes & Lorenzo Martin

Gm⁷

E♭add⁹

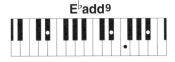

B♭

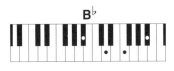

G♭maj7aug

E♭maj⁹

Intro

     ‖: Gm⁷ E♭add⁹ | B♭ G♭maj7aug |
Come on!

   Gm⁷ E♭maj⁹ | B♭ G♭maj7aug :‖
Ooh!   Yeah!

Verse 1

Gm⁷   E♭add⁹ B♭   G♭maj7aug
 I call you up whenever things go wrong.

Gm⁷   E♭maj⁹   B♭   G♭maj7aug
 You're always there, you are my shoulder to cry on.

Gm⁷   E♭maj⁹   B♭   G♭maj7aug
 I can't believe it took me quite so long

  Gm⁷   E♭maj⁹
To take the forbidden step.

    B♭   G♭maj7aug
Is this something I might regret?

Bridge 1

Gm⁷   E♭add⁹
 (Come on, come on,)

B♭   G♭maj7aug Gm⁷
 Nothing ventured, nothing gained.

  E♭maj⁹ B♭
(You are the one.)

      G♭maj7aug   Gm⁷
A lonely heart that can't be tamed.

   E♭maj⁹ B♭
(Come on, come on,)

      G♭maj7aug Gm⁷ E♭maj⁹
I'm hoping that you feel the same,

    B♭   G♭maj7aug
This is something I can't forget.

Chorus 1

Gm7　　　　　**E♭add9**　　　　　　　　　**B♭**
　I thought that we would just be friends.
　　　　　　G♭maj7aug
Things will never be the same again.
Gm7　　　　　**E♭maj9**　　　　　　　**B♭**
　It's just the beginning, it's not the end.
　　　　　　G♭maj7aug
Things will never be the same again.
Gm7　　　**E♭maj9**　　　**B♭**
　It's not a secret anymore,
　　　　　G♭maj7aug
Now we've opened up the door.
Gm7　　　**E♭maj9**　　　　　　**B♭**
　Starting tonight and from now on
　　　　　　G♭maj7aug
We'll never, never be the same again.
Gm7　　　　　**E♭add9**　　**B♭**
　(Never be the same again.)
G♭maj7aug
Never be the same again.
Gm7　　　　　**E♭maj9**　　**B♭**　　**G♭maj7aug**
　(Never be the same again.)

Verse 2

Gm7　　　　　**E♭add9**　　　　　**B♭**　　　**G♭maj7aug**
　Now I know that we were close before,
Gm7　　　　**E♭maj9**　　**B♭**　　　　　　**G♭maj7aug**
　I'm glad I realised I need you so much more.
Gm7　　　　**E♭maj9**　　　　　　**B♭**　　　**G♭maj7aug**
　And I don't care what everyone will say
　　Gm7　　　　　**E♭maj9**
It's about you and me
　　　　B♭　　　**G♭maj7aug**
And we'll never be the same again.

Chorus 2

As Chorus 1

27

Middle *(spoken)*

Nite and day
Gm⁷   **E♭maj⁹**   **B♭**
Black beach sand to red clay to the US to UK,
                   G♭maj⁷aug   **Gm⁷**
NYC to LA from sidewalks to highways.
                               E♭maj⁹
See, it'll never be the same, what I'm sayin'
       B♭
My mind frame never changed
            G♭maj⁷aug
Till you came and rearranged.
       N.C.
But sometimes it seems completely forbidden

To discover those feelings that we kept so well hidden.

Where there's no competition

And you render my condition,

Though improbable, it's not impossible

For a love that could be unstoppable, but wait.

A fine line's between fate and destiny.

Do you believe in the things that were just meant to be?

When you tell me the stories of your quest for me,

Picturesque is the picture you paint effortlessly.
         Gm⁷   **E♭add⁹**
And as our energies mix and begin to multiply,
      B♭   **G♭maj⁷aug**
Everyday situations they start to simplify.
   Gm⁷   **E♭maj⁹**
So things will never be the same between you and I
    B♭   **G♭maj⁷aug**
We intertwined our life forces and now we're unified.

Chorus 3

Gm⁷   **E♭add⁹**   **B♭**
   I thought that we would just be friends.

           G♭maj⁷aug
Things will never be the same again.

Gm⁷   **E♭maj⁹**   **B♭**
   It's just the beginning, it's not the end.

           G♭maj⁷aug
Things will never be the same again.

Gm⁷   **E♭maj⁹**   **B♭**
   It's not a secret anymore,

           G♭maj⁷aug
Now we've opened up the door.

Gm⁷   **E♭maj⁹**   **B♭**
   Starting tonight and from now on

           G♭maj⁷aug
We'll never, never be the same again.

Gm⁷   **E♭maj⁹**

B♭   **G♭maj⁷aug**
   And things will never be the same again.

Gm⁷   **E♭maj⁹** | **B♭**

G♭maj⁷aug
Never be the same again.

Oops! ... I Did It Again

Words & Music by Max Martin & Rami Yacoub

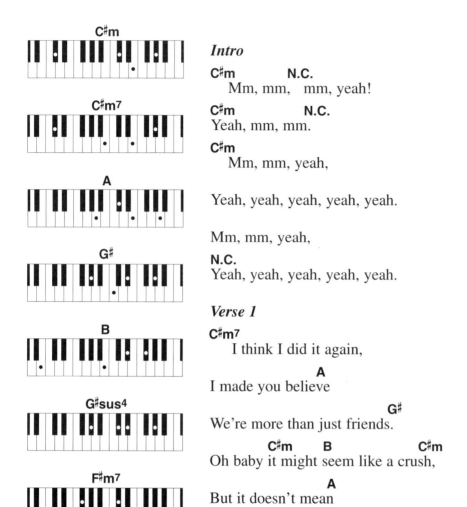

Intro

C#m   N.C.
 Mm, mm, mm, yeah!

C#m   N.C.
Yeah, mm, mm.

C#m
 Mm, mm, yeah,

Yeah, yeah, yeah, yeah, yeah.

Mm, mm, yeah,

N.C.
Yeah, yeah, yeah, yeah, yeah.

Verse 1

C#m7
 I think I did it again,

     A
I made you believe

        G#
We're more than just friends.

    C#m B   C#m
Oh baby it might seem like a crush,

       A
But it doesn't mean

      G#sus4 G#
That I'm serious.

     F#m7 G#7
Cos to lose all my senses,

    A   B
That is just so typically me.

Oh baby, baby.

Chorus 1

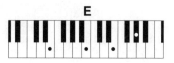

E

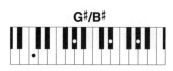

G#/B#

C#m   G#   C#m
Oops!…I did it again,

 B   E
I played with your heart,

  B   E
Got a' lost in the game.

  B G#/B#
Oh baby, baby

C#m   G#   C#m
Oops! You think I'm in love,

   B   E
That I'm sent from above.

  G#   C#m
I'm not that innocent.

Verse 2

C#m7
 You see, my problem is this,

       A
I'm dreaming away,

        G#
Wishing that heroes they truly exist.

C#m B   C#m
I cry watching the days,

       A
Can't you see I'm a fool

    G#sus4 G#
In so many ways.

   F#m7   G#7
But to lose all my senses,

   A   B
That is just so typically me.

Oh baby, baby.

Chorus 2

As Chorus 1

more chords overleaf…

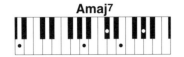
Amaj⁷

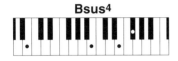
Bsus⁴

Link

C♯m
   Mm, mm, yeah,

Yeah, yeah, yeah, yeah, yeah.

Mm, mm, yeah,
N.C.
Yeah, yeah, yeah, yeah, yeah.

Middle (spoken)

Amaj⁷
"All aboard!"

         B
"Britney, before you go,

there's something I want you to have."

Amaj⁷   **Bsus⁴**
"Oh, it's beautiful, but wait a minute. Isn't this…?"

B
"Yes it is."

Amaj⁷
"But I thought the old lady dropped it into the ocean

B
in the end."

            G♯   **C♯m**
"Well baby, I went down and got it for ya."

"Oh, you shouldn't have."

Chorus 3

    B C♯m   **B**   **E**
Oops! I   did it again to your heart.

     B **E**
Got a' lost in this game.

  B   **G♯/B♯**
Oh ba--by,

C♯m   **G♯** **C♯m**   **B**   **E**
  Oops! You think that I'm sent from above.

   A   **B**
I'm not that innocent.

Chorus 4

```
C#m      G#        C#m
Oops! I did it again,
       B                    E
I've played with your heart,
           B              E
Got a' lost in the game.
       B      G#/B#
Oh baby, baby
C#m        G#          C#m
Oops! You think I'm in love,
             B              E
That I'm sent from above.
       G#
I'm not that innocent.
```

Chorus 5

```
C#m      G#        C#m
Oops! I did it again,
       B                    E
I played with your heart,
          B              E
Got a' lost in the game.
      B      G#/B#
Oh baby, baby
C#m        G#            C#m
Oops! You think I'm in love,
             B              E
That I'm sent from above.
       G#        N.C.
I'm not that innocent.
```

Rise

Words & Music by Bob Dylan, Gabrielle, Ferdy Unger-Hamilton & Ollie Dagois

A♭

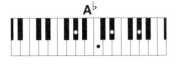

E♭

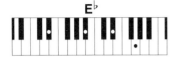

B♭m7

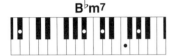

Intro

A♭ E♭ B♭m7   A♭ E♭ B♭m7
Mm.   Mm.

Verse 1

A♭   E♭   B♭m7
I know that it's over,
A♭   E♭   B♭m7
But I can't believe we're through.
A♭   E♭   B♭m7
They say that time's a healer, yeah,
A♭   E♭   B♭m7
And I'm better without you.
                    A♭   E♭
It's gonna take time, I know,
                B♭m7
But I'll get over you.

Chorus 1

                A♭   E♭
Look at my life, look in my heart,
        B♭m7
I have seen them fall apart,
                A♭   E♭   B♭m7
Now I'm ready   to rise again.
                    A♭   E♭
Just look at my hopes, look at my dreams,
            B♭m7
I'm building bridges from the scenes.
                A♭   E♭   B♭m7
Now I'm ready   to rise again.

Link

A♭ E♭ B♭m7
Mm.

Verse 2

A♭ **E♭** **B♭m7**
 Caught up in my thinking,
A♭ **E♭**   **B♭m7**
 Like a prisoner in my mind.
A♭ **E♭**   **B♭m7**
 You pose so many questions
A♭ **E♭**   **B♭m7**
 That the truth is hard to find.
      A♭ **E♭**
I'd better think twice, I know
    B♭m7
That I'll get over you.

Chorus 2

As Chorus 1

Verse 3

A♭ **E♭**   **B♭m7**
 Much time has passed between us, mm,
A♭   **E♭**   **B♭m7**
 Do you still think of me at all?
A♭ **E♭**   **B♭m7**
 My world of broken promises
A♭   **E♭**   **B♭m7**
 Where you won't catch me when I fall.

Chorus 3

As Chorus 1

Outro

‖:   **A♭**   **E♭**
 I'm gonna make it alright, yes I'm gonna rise
   B♭m7
Make it alright,

I'm gonna be who I wanna be, yeah
A♭ **E♭** **B♭m7** :‖ *Repeat to fade*
Baby, yeah, yeah.

She's The One

Words and Music by Karl Wallinger

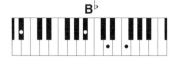

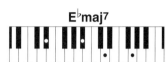

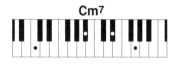

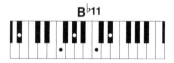

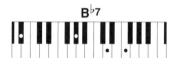

Intro

| B♭ | E♭maj7 | B♭ | E♭maj7 ‖

Verse 1

    B♭   E♭maj7
I was her, she was me,
      B♭   E♭maj7
We were one, we were free.
         Cm7   F7
And if there's somebody calling me on
      B♭ E♭maj7
She's the one.
       Cm7   F7
If there's somebody calling me on
      B♭ | E♭maj7
She's the one.

Verse 2

       B♭   E♭maj7
We were young, we were wrong,
     B♭   E♭maj7
We were fine all along.
       Cm7   F7
If there's somebody calling me on
      B♭ | B♭11 B♭7
She's the one.

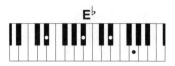

Eb

Middle

Eb
  When you get to where you wanna go

And you know the things you wanna know,
      Bb   Bb11   Bb7
You're smiling.
Eb
  When you said what you wanna say

And you know the way you wanna play, yeah
Cm   F11 F
  You'll be so high, you'll be fly-ing.

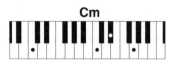

Cm

Verse 3
         Bb   Ebmaj7
Though the sea will be strong,
    Bb   Ebmaj7
I know we'll carry on.
           Cm7   F7
Cos if there's somebody calling me on
        Bb   Ebmaj7
She's the one.
       Cm7   F7
If there's somebody calling me on
      Bb |Bb11   Bb7
She's the one.

F11

Middle

Eb
  When you get to where you wanna go

And you know the things you wanna know,
      Bb   Bb11   Bb7
You're smiling.
Eb
  When you said what you wanna say

And you know the way you wanna say, yeah
Cm   F11 F
  You'll be so high, you'll be fly-ing.

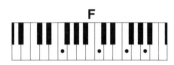

F

more chords overleaf…

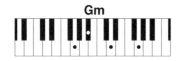

Gm

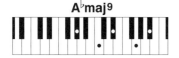

A♭maj9

Verse 4

      B♭   **E♭maj7**
I was her, she was me,
         B♭   **E♭maj7**
We were one, we were free.
                Cm7   **F7**
And if there's somebody calling me on
         B♭   **B♭7**
She's the one.

Ending

            Cm7   **F7**
If there's somebody calling me on
         B♭   **B♭7**
She's the one.
            Cm7   **F7**
If there's somebody calling me on
   Gm
She's the one.
          E♭
Yes, she's the one.
            Cm7   **F7**
If there's somebody calling me on
   Gm
She's the one.
        A♭maj9
She's the one.
            Cm7   **F7**
If there's somebody calling me on
   Gm
She's the one.
      E♭
She's the one.
            Cm7   **F**
If there's somebody calling me on
        B♭ |**E♭maj7** |**B♭** |**E♭maj7**
She's the one.
        B♭
She's the one.

Still

Words by Macy Gray. Music by Jeremy Ruzumna & Bill Esses

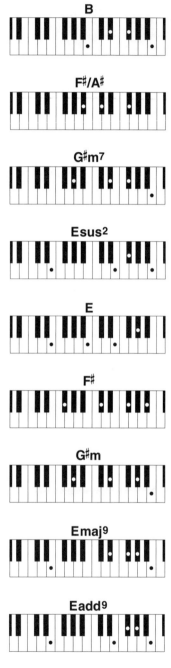

Verse 1

B

  In my last years with him

      F#/A#

There were bruises on my face.

    G#m7

In my dawn and new day

  Esus2

I finally got away.

B

  But my head's all messed up

     F#/A#

And he knows just what to say.

    G#m7

No more dawn and new days,

   E

I'm goin' back to stay.

    F# **G#m**   **Emaj9**

So why   say bye bye

      F# **G#m7**   **Eadd9**

When it only makes me cry?

Chorus 1

   B

I still light up like a candle burnin'

    F#/A#

When he calls me up.

 G#m7

I still melt down like a candle burnin'

   Esus2

Every time we touch.

      F#

Oh say what you will,

   G#m   **E**

He does me wrong and I should be gone.

more chords overleaf…

B
But I   still be lovin' you baby

And it's much too much.

Verse 2
B
We are going down
       F#/A#
Cos you're always getting high.
       G#m7
And your crumbs of lovin'
  Esus2
No longer get me by.
B
  Wow! It gets better
       F#/A#
Every time that we get high,
       G#m7
Then your crumbs of lovin'
      E
They somehow get me by.
    F# **G#m**   **Emaj9**
Why   say bye bye
       F# **G#m7**   **Eadd9**
When it only makes me cry?

Chorus 2
  B
I still light up like a candle burnin'
       F#/A#
When he calls me up.
  G#m7
I still melt down like a candle burnin'
      Esus2
Every time we touch.
    B
I still light up like a candle burnin'
       F#/A#
When he calls me up.

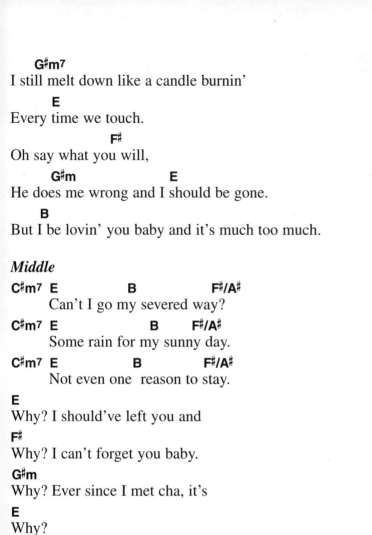

G#m7
I still melt down like a candle burnin'
     E
Every time we touch.
          F#
Oh say what you will,
    G#m   **E**
He does me wrong and I should be gone.
   B
But I be lovin' you baby and it's much too much.

Middle

C#m7 E   **B**   **F#/A#**
    Can't I go my severed way?
C#m7 E   **B**   **F#/A#**
    Some rain for my sunny day.
C#m7 E   **B**   **F#/A#**
    Not even one reason to stay.
E
Why? I should've left you and
F#
Why? I can't forget you baby.
G#m
Why? Ever since I met cha, it's
E
Why?

Break

|: **B** | **F#/A#** | **G#m7** | **E**   :|
   Still…

Chorus 3

As Chorus 2

The Time Is Now

Words & Music by Mark Brydon & Roisin Murphy

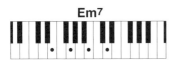

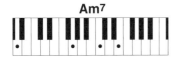

Intro

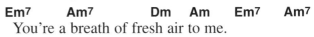

| N.C. | Em⁷ Am⁷ Dm| | Am | Em⁷ Am⁷ |

| Dm Am | Em⁷ Am⁷ | F | G | |

Verse 1

Dm   Am
  You're my last breath,

Em⁷   Am⁷   Dm Am   Em⁷   Am⁷
  You're a breath of fresh air to me.

Dm   Am
  Hi, I'm empty,

Em⁷ Am⁷   Dm Am   Em⁷   Am⁷
    So tell me you care for me.

Dm   Am
  You're the first thing

Em⁷ Am⁷   Dm Am   Em⁷   Am⁷
  And the last thing on my mind.

Dm Am   Em⁷ Am⁷ F   G
  In your arms I feel   sunshine.

Verse 2

Dm Am
  On a promise,

Em⁷ Am⁷ Dm Am   Em⁷   Am⁷
  A daydream yet to come.

Dm   Am
  Time is upon us

Em⁷ Am⁷   Dm Am   Em⁷   Am⁷
  Oh, but the night is young.

Dm   Am
  Flowers blossom

Em⁷ Am⁷ Dm Am   Em⁷   Am⁷
  In the   winter time.

Dm Am   Em⁷ Am⁷ F   G
  In your arms I feel   sunshine.

Chorus 1

Dm   Am/E   Em/G   F/A Em/A
   Give up yourself unto the moment,

Dm Am   Em/G F/A Em/A
   The time is now.

Dm   Am/E   Em/G F/A Em/A
   Give up yourself unto the moment,

F   G6
   Let's make this moment last.

Verse 3

Dm   Am   Em7   Am7
   You may find yourself

Dm   Am   Em7   Am7
   Out on a limb for me.

Dm   Am
   Could you accept it as

F   G
   Part of your destiny?

Dm Am   Em7 Am7
   I give all I have,

Dm Am   Em7   Am
   But it's not enough.

Dm Am   Em7   Am7
   And my patience are shot,

F   G
   So I'm calling your bluff.

Chorus 2

Dm   Am/E   Em/G   F/A Em/A
   Give up yourself unto the moment,

Dm Am   Em/G Fsus4 Em/A
   The time is now.

Dm   Am   Em/G F/A Em/A
   Give up yourself unto the moment,

F   G6
Let's make this moment last.

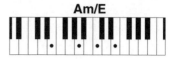

Am/E

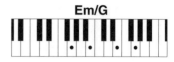

Em/G

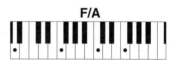

F/A

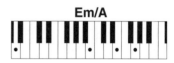

Em/A

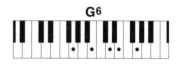

G6

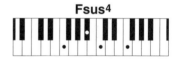

Fsus4

more chords overleaf…

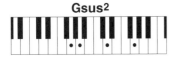
Gsus2

Dmadd11/A

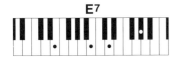
E7

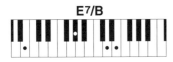
E7/B

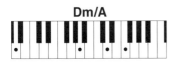
Dm/A

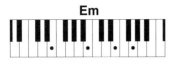
Em

F/C

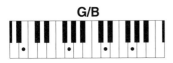
G/B

Asus2/E

Chorus 3

Dm   **Am/E**   **Em/G**   **F/A**   **Em/A**
   Give up yourself unto the moment,

Dm Am   **Em/G Fsus4 Em/A**
   The time is now.

Dm   **Am**   **Em/G F/A**   **Em/A**
   Give up yourself unto the moment,

F   **G6**   **Gsus2**
  Let's make this moment last.

Middle

Dmadd11/A   **E7**
    And we gave it time,

E7/B   **Am**
   All eyes are on the clock.

Dm/A   **Am**
   Time takes too much time,

Em   **Am**
   Please make the waiting stop.

Dm Am
    And the atmosphere is charged,

Dm Am
    And in you I trust.

N.C.
And I feel no fear as I

F/C   **G/B**
   Do as I must.

Chorus 4

Dm   **Am/E**   **Em/G**   **F/A**   **Em/A**
   Give up yourself unto the moment,

Dm Am   **Em/G F/A**   **Em/A**
   The time is now.

Dm   **Am**   **Em/G F/A**   **Em/A**
   Give up yourself unto the moment,

F   **G6**
   Let's make this moment last.

Verse 4

Dm   Am   Em7   Am7
 Tempted by fate

Dm   Am   Em7   Am7
 And I won't hesitate.

Dm   Am
 The time is now,

F   G
 Let's make this moment last.

Dm Am   Em7   Am7
      The night is young,

Dm Am   Em7   Am
      The time is now.

Dm Am   Em7   Am7   F   G
      Let's make this moment last.

Chorus 5

Dm   Am/E   Em/G   F/A Em/A
 Give up yourself unto the moment,

Dm Am   Em/G Fsus4 Em/A
  The time is now.

Dm   Am   Em/G F/A   Em/A
 Give up yourself unto the moment,

F   G6   Asus2/E
 Let's make this moment   last.

Outro

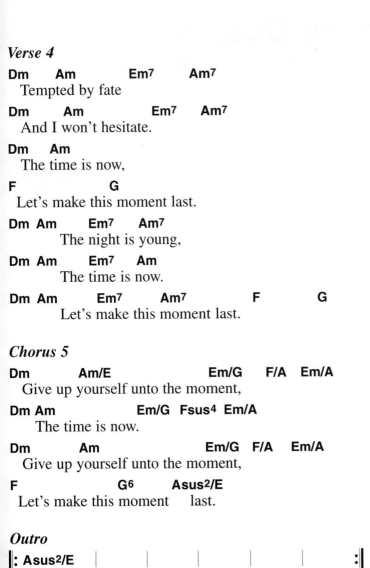

Repeat to fade

Why Does It Always Rain On Me?

Words & Music by Fran Healy

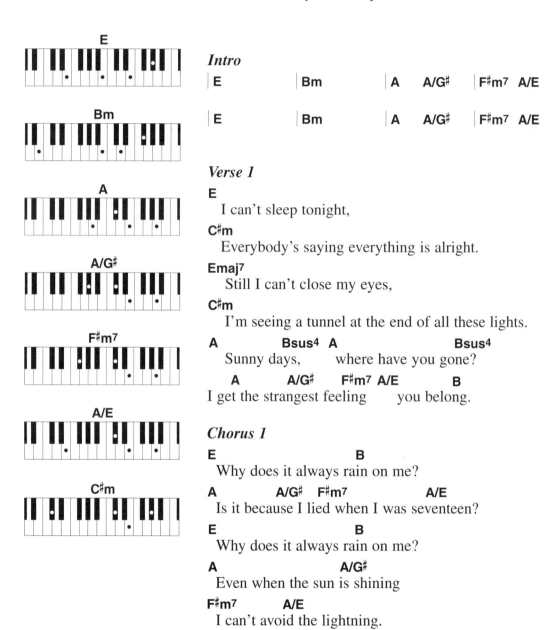

Intro

| E | Bm | A | A/G# | F#m7 | A/E |

| E | Bm | A | A/G# | F#m7 | A/E |

Verse 1

E
   I can't sleep tonight,
C#m
   Everybody's saying everything is alright.
Emaj7
   Still I can't close my eyes,
C#m
   I'm seeing a tunnel at the end of all these lights.
A   Bsus4 A   Bsus4
   Sunny days,   where have you gone?
     A   A/G#   F#m7 A/E   B
I get the strangest feeling   you belong.

Chorus 1

E   B
   Why does it always rain on me?
A   A/G# F#m7   A/E
   Is it because I lied when I was seventeen?
E   B
   Why does it always rain on me?
A   A/G#
   Even when the sun is shining
F#m7   A/E
   I can't avoid the lightning.

Verse 2

E
  I can't stand myself,

C♯m
  I'm being held up by invisible men.

Emaj⁷
  Still life on a shelf

C♯m
  When I got my mind on something else.

A   **Bsus⁴ A**   **Bsus⁴**
  Sunny days,   where have you gone?

     A   **A/G♯** **F♯m⁷ A/E**   **B**
I get the strangest feeling   you belong.

Chorus 2

As Chorus 1

Link 1

   C♯m   **E/B**
Oh, where did the blue sky go?

    C♯m   **E/B**   **D**   **D/C♯**
Oh, why is it raining so?_____

Bm⁷ D/A Bsus⁴   B
  It's so cold._____

Verse 3

As Verse 1

Chorus 3

As Chorus 1

Link 2

    C♯m   **E/B**
Oh,   where did the blue sky go?

    C♯m   **E/B**   **D**   **D/C♯**
Oh,   why is it raining so?_____

Bm⁷ D/A Bsus⁴   B
  It's so cold._____

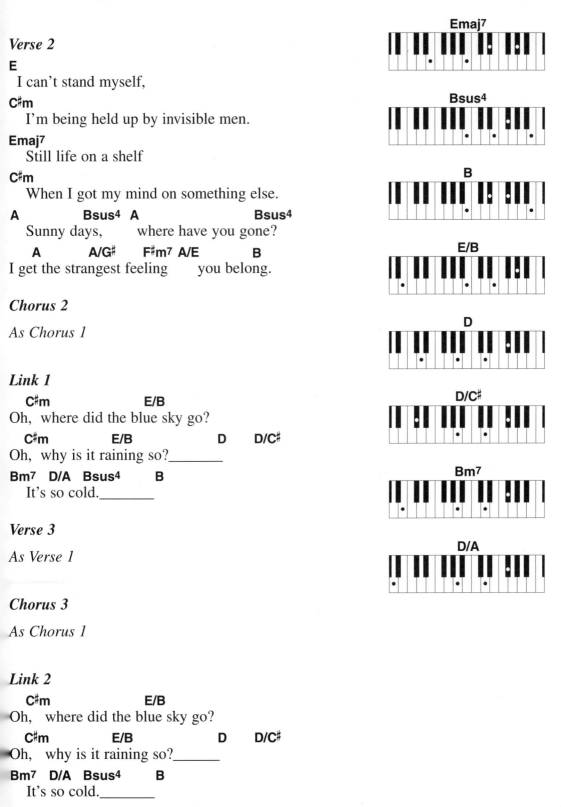

Emaj⁷

Bsus⁴

B

E/B

D

D/C♯

Bm⁷

D/A

more chords overleaf...

E6

Chorus 4

E   B
  Why does it always rain on me?

A   A/G♯   F♯m7   A/E
  Is it because I lied when I was seventeen?

E   B
  Why does it always rain on me?

A   A/G♯
  Even when the sun is shining

F♯m7   A/E
  I can't avoid the lightning.

Ending

E   Bm   A   A/G♯
  Why does it always rain on me?

F♯m7   A/E

E6   Bm
  Why does it always rain on…

A   A/G♯ | F♯m7   A/E
                       oh.